Dragon Island

Written by
Maggie Freeman

Illustrated by
Brian Fitzgerald

"I've brought you a present from America,"
says Uncle Jim.
"Thank you," says Alex.
Alex and his friend Flora unwrap the purple paper
with its pirate flags.

"What is it?" asks Flora.
"It's a green stone," says Alex.
"It's an island," says Uncle Jim.
"Silly island," says Alex.
"It's a magic island," says Uncle Jim. "Put it in your paddling pool. See what happens."

Alex puts the tiny island in his paddling pool and it …

… floats and grows and GROWS.

Alex and Flora paddle out to the island. The water is soon as deep as their knees.

Then they have to swim. They are good swimmers, because they go to swimming lessons on Saturday mornings.
"I'll race you," says Flora.
But Alex wins.

Alex comes to a beach and steps up on the sand.
"Come on, Flora," he says.
Flora stands on the sand.
"What's that noise?" she says.
It's a sad noise, as if someone is crying.

"Look," says Alex.
At the top of the beach is a tree.
Behind the tree is a …

"What is it?" says Flora.
"It's a little dragon," says Alex.
"What's your name, little dragon?" says Flora.
"My name's Danny," sobs the dragon.
"What's the matter, Danny?" says Alex. "Why are you crying?"

"My mum told me to come to the island and find my treasure," Danny sobs. "But I can't find it."
"Do you have a treasure map?" says Alex.
"Yes," sobs Danny. "My mum gave it to me. But I can't read."

"Show it to us, then," says Flora. "I'm seven, and I can read."
"I'm six and a half," says Alex. "I can read too."

The dragon opens his backpack, and takes out the treasure map. He gives it to Alex and Flora.

"It's a map of this island," says Alex. "Look, here's the beach where we're standing."
"This big **X** marks the spot where the treasure is buried," says Flora. "If we climb this big hill and go down the other side, we'll find the treasure. It's buried here, by these rocks."

All three of them climb the hill. They go down the other side.

But what do they see down by the rocks?
"EEEK," squeaks Flora.
"SCARY," says Alex.

Down by the rocks are SIX CROCODILES WITH SNAPPING TEETH!

Danny starts to cry again. "I can't get my treasure," he sobs.
"Oh yes, you can," says Flora. "You can chase the crocodiles away."
"I can?" says Danny.
"Yes," says Flora. "Be brave."

"OK," says Danny. He runs down the hill. "ROAR!" he shouts. "ROAR, ROAR!"
The crocodiles look up and see him.
"EEEK!" they squeak. "SCARY!" They run away.

"Hooray," says Alex. "Now if we had some spades, we could dig up the treasure."

"I've got spades in my backpack," says Danny.

Alex and Flora and Danny soon dig up an iron chest.

Danny has the key to open it. "Hooray!" he says. "My treasure at last!"

They look at the shiny gold and bright jewels.

Danny picks out a gold ring and gives it to Alex and Flora.
"Thank your for helping me," he says.

Alex and Flora run back to the beach.
They swim back to the paddling pool and step out on the grass.

Uncle Jim is waiting for them.

"We've brought you a present from Dragon Island," says Alex.
"It's a ring," says Uncle Jim.
"It's a magic ring," says Flora.
"Silly ring," says Uncle Jim. "What can it do?"
"Put it on your finger," says Alex. "See what happens."
"It's too little for my finger," says Uncle Jim. "You put it on **your** finger. **You** see what happens."